LEARN TOGETHER
MATHS

D1741151

MATHS TESTS

400 questions
to help your child with
SUBTRACTION

Richard Dawson

Macmillan
Children's Books

First published 1997 by Macmillan Children's Books
a division of Macmillan Publishers Limited
25 Eccleston Place, London SW1W 9NF
and Basingstoke

Associated companies throughout the world

ISBN 0 330 35161 3

9 8 7 6 5 4 3 2 1

A CIP catalogue record for this book is available from the British Library.

Typeset by Macmillan Children's Books. Printed by Henry Ling Ltd, The Dorset Press, Dorchester.

	6985	2	14516	3	25018	4	36984
−	3539	−	9953	−	16929	−	9568

	44206	6	50483	7	59743	8	73504
−	29196	−	31579	−	10959	−	59839

	80024	10	77283	11	94762	12	100036
−	56375	−	9895	−	38529	−	29759

13	122086	14	162397	15	120286	16	208530
−	94277	−	56985	−	79049	−	68395

17	8903	18	4826	19	84313	20	62573
−	7019	−	3714	−	22956	−	35142

3

21	8008	22	28027	23	25254	24	49436
−	5976	−	10994	−	19799	−	29648

25	58308	26	170050	27	379827	28	99385
−	37992	−	59465	−	220596	−	74658

29	632419	30	849462	31	186607	32	207957
−	363986	−	79945	−	97845	−	149932

33	204947	34	576596	35	409395	36	924497
−	148957	−	195708	−	387796	−	597598

37	297208	38	452803	39	15012	40	10082
−	35819	−	132456	−	6094	−	9328

41 £	42 £	43 £	44 £
9.46	22.68	41.23	74.28
− 3.90	− 15.86	− 39.97	− 39.93

45 £	46 £	47 £	48 £
99.33	248.52	283.94	364.27
− 72.64	− 69.65	− 250.26	− 97.84

49 £	50 £	51 £	52 £
429.65	496.79	495.07	600.00
− 296.75	− 399.68	− 446.29	− 518.75

53 £	54 £	55 £	56 £
185.36	236.00	91.26	26.48
− 107.49	− 168.97	− 87.60	− 10.79

57 £	58 £	59 £	60 £
65.13	89.74	101.27	109.59
− 28.84	− 51.26	− 45.85	− 95.81

61 £
    74.18
  - 68.29
  _____

62 £
    123.64
  - 85.17
  _____

63 £
    100.73
  - 98.91
  _____

64 £
    139.74
  -125.01
  _____

65 £
    326.22
  -108.00
  _____

66 £
    267.47
  -149.39
  _____

67 £
    675.87
  -287.60
  _____

68 £
    806.48
  -352.52
  _____

69 £
    683.63
  -509.85
  _____

70 £
    957.49
  -905.85
  _____

71 £
    50.36
  - 42.48
  _____

72 £
    78.37
  - 38.91
  _____

73 £
    153.01
  - 78.18
  _____

74 £
    196.87
  -152.96
  _____

75 £
    236.35
  - 89.75
  _____

76 £
    467.15
  -253.93
  _____

77 £
    744.47
  -496.58
  _____

78 £
    950.10
  - 92.08
  _____

79 £
    1398.48
  - 486.57
  _____

80 £
    1500.08
  -1496.10
  _____

81	min	sec	82	min	sec	83	min	sec	84	min	sec
	5	50		9	49		7	20		10	45
−	3	30	−	6	32	−	5	50	−	4	59

85	hrs	min	86	hrs	min	87	hrs	min	88	hrs	min
	8	45		6	45		10	18		12	45
−	5	35	−	5	28	−	7	35	−	8	52

89	days	hrs	90	days	hrs	91	days	hrs	92	days	hrs
	19	22		32	22		46	4		33	10
−	3	9	−	17	15	−	22	21	−	14	16

93	wks	days	94	wks	days	95	wks	days	96	wks	days
	17	5		14	2		10	0		16	5
−	9	3	−	4	7	−	3	6	−	9	6

97	wks	days	98	wks	days	99	wks	days	100	wks	days
	35	3		8	3		6	5		9	6
−	4	6	−	4	1	−	2	0	−	5	4

101	hrs	min	sec
	15	58	24
−	6	21	49

102	hrs	min	sec
	18	15	36
−	12	26	58

103	hrs	min	sec
	17	19	30
−	11	37	42

104	days	hrs	min
	18	20	7
−	15	10	30

105	days	hrs	min
	36	8	28
−	27	19	50

106	days	hrs	min
	44	12	39
−	12	15	55

107	wks	days	hrs
	15	4	22
−	7	6	14

108	wks	days	hrs
	27	6	12
−	10	4	19

109	wks	days	hrs
	32	0	12
−	16	3	17

110	wks	days	hrs
	29	3	10
−	11	6	14

111	wks	days	hrs
	36	4	14
−	19	5	16

112	wks	days	hrs
	44	6	16
−	22	5	9

113	wks	days	hrs
	11	1	17
−	10	6	20

114	wks	days	hrs
	19	3	6
−	14	3	19

115	wks	days	hrs
	16	2	12
−	8	5	13

116	days	hrs	min
	9	8	57
−	7	12	34

117	days	hrs	min
	11	22	16
−	10	14	12

118	days	hrs	min
	16	1	56
−	8	17	20

119	hrs	min	sec
	4	7	28
−	3	10	14

120	hrs	min	sec
	6	15	47
−	5	29	18

121		g
		639
−		493

122	kg	g
	2	0
−		340

123	kg	g
	4	72
−		150

124	kg	g
	14	400
−	6	700

125	tns	kg
	8	0
	2	500

126	tns	kg
	10	400
−	3	40

127	kg	g
	14	740
−	9	620

128	tns	kg
	17	8
−	14	115

129	tns	kg
	4	100
−	3	500

130	kg	g
	6	950
−	3	400

131	tns	kg
	5	200
−	2	300

132	kg	g
	4	750
−	2	500

133	kg	g
	9	250
−		750

134	kg	g
	8	0
−	1	500

135	kg	g
	7	500
−	5	750

136	kg	g
	12	180
−	9	680

137	tns	kg
	13	550
−	10	705

138	tns	kg
	11	490
−	6	360

139	kg	g
	11	500
−	5	160

140	tns	kg
	11	50
−	4	200

	141	kg	g		142	tns	kg		143	kg	g		144	kg	g
		27	675			20	483			30	835			64	841
	−	13	740		−	14	85		−	29	253		−	56	710

	145	kg	g		146	tns	kg		147	kg	g		148	tns	kg
		74	41			70	196			107	926			131	450
	−	56	710		−	36	208		−	84	476		−	97	694

	149	kg	g		150	tns	kg		151	kg	g		152	tns	kg
		76	510			97	446			9	459			72	84
	−	49	750		−	38	942		−	7	626		−	21	00

	153	kg	g		154	kg	g		155	tns	kg		156	tns	kg
		145	756			134	215			118	150			31	600
	−	97	357		−	114	529		−	67	458		−	10	250

	157	kg	g		158	tns	kg		159	kg	g		160	tns	kg
		48	700			78	939			89	621			39	580
	−	28	580		−	33	830		−	57	476		−	23	140

NOTE TO PARENTS

Subtraction is one of the key rules of computation. It can be made straightforward by taking the logical approach.

Look at this sum . . .

```
  5 0
 -3 4
  2 4
```
is the answer often written by children.

Look at this sequence . . .

$$
\begin{array}{cccc}
50 & \overset{4}{\cancel{5}}0 & \overset{4}{\cancel{5}}{}^{1}0 & \overset{4}{\cancel{5}}{}^{1}0 \\
-34 & -34 & -34 & -34 \\
 & & 6 & 16
\end{array}
$$

This process of breaking the sum down into simpler constituents is called *decomposition* and it necessitates a good understanding of place value. However once this concept and method of working is understood, subtraction is easy!

The only tricky times are when the sum is not in base 10. Remember when working with time that there are 60 seconds in a minute, 60 minutes in an hour and 24 hours in a day.

There are 400 questions in this book; I hope you get most of the answers right! Have fun.

Answers

1. 3446	36. 326899	71. 7.88	106. 31days 20hrs 44min
2. 4563	37. 261389	72. 39.46	107. 7wks 5days 8hrs
3. 8089	38. 320347	73. 74.83	108. 17wks 1day 17hrs
4. 27416	39. 8918	74. 43.91	109. 15wks 3days 19hrs
5. 15010	40. 754	75. 146.60	110. 17wks 3days 20hrs
6. 18904	41. 5.56	76. 213.22	111. 16wks 5days 22hrs
7. 48784	42. 6.82	77. 247.89	112. 22wks 1day 7hrs
8. 13665	43. 1.26	78. 858.02	113. 1day 21hrs
9. 23649	44. 34.35	79. 911.91	114. 4wks 6days 11hrs
10. 67388	45. 26.69	80. 3.98	115. 7wks 3days 23hrs
11. 56233	46. 178.87	81. 2min 20sec	116. 1day 20hrs 23min
12. 70277	47. 33.68	82. 3min 17sec	117. 1day 8hrs 4min
13. 27809	48. 266.43	83. 1min 30sec	118. 7days 8hrs 36min
14. 105412	49. 132.90	84. 5min 46sec	119. 57min 14sec
15. 41237	50. 97.11	85. 3hrs 10min	120. 46min 29sec
16. 140135	51. 48.78	86. 1hrs 17min	121. 146g
17. 1884	52. 81.25	87. 2hrs 43min	122. 1kg 660g
18. 1112	53. 77.87	88. 3hrs 53min	123. 3kg 922g
19. 61357	54. 67.03	89. 16days 13hrs	124. 7kg 700g
20. 27431	55. 3.66	90. 15days 7hrs	125. 5tonnes 500kg
21. 2032	56. 15.69	91. 23days 7hrs	126. 7tonnes 360kg
22. 17033	57. 36.29	92. 18days 18hrs	127. 5tonnes 120kg
23. 5455	58. 38.48	93. 8wks 2days	128. 2tonnes 893kg
24. 19788	59. 55.42	94. 9wks 2days	129. 600kg
25. 20316	60. 13.78	95. 6wks 1days	130. 3kg 550g
26. 110585	61. 5.89	96. 6wks 6days	131. 2tonnes 900kg
27. 159231	62. 38.47	97. 30wks 4days	132. 2kg 250g
28. 24727	63. 1.82	98. 4wks 2days	133. 8kg 500g
29. 268433	64. 14.73	99. 4wks 5days	134. 6kg 500g
30. 769517	65. 218.22	100. 4wks 2days	135. 1kg 750g
31. 88762	66. 118.08	101. 9hrs 36min 35sec	136. 2kg 500g
32. 58025	67. 388.27	102. 5hrs 48min 38sec	137. 2tonnes 845kg
33. 55990	68. 453.96	103. 5hrs 41min 48sec	138. 5tonnes 130kg
34. 380888	69. 173.78	104. 3days 9hrs 37min	139. 6kg 340g
35. 21599	70. 51.64	105. 8days 12hrs 38min	140. 6kg 850g

Answers (continued)

141. 13kg 935g	175. 2ltrs 190ml	209. 1km 220m
142. 6tonnes 398kg	176. 6ltrs 830ml	210. 5km 240m
143. 1kg 582g	177. 12ltrs 30ml	211. 5km 620m
144. 8kg 131g	178. 7ltrs 900ml	212. 70m
145. 17kg 331g	179. 5ltrs 144ml	213. 4m 18cm
146. 33tonnes 988kg	180. 11ltrs 560ml	214. 4m 50cm
147. 23kg 450g	181. 0ltrs 784ml	215. 3m 79cm
148. 33tonnes 756kg	182. 8ltrs 400ml	216. 9m 41cm
149. 26kg 760g	183. 7ltrs 519ml	217. 3km 290m
150. 58tonnes 504kg	184. 11ltrs 385ml	218. 1km 150m
151. 1kg 833g	185. 13ltrs 542ml	219. 4m 32cm
152. 51tonnes 84kg	186. 42ltrs 211ml	220. 63cm
153. 48kg 399g	187. 23ltrs 425ml	221. 13km 150m
154. 19kg 686g	188. 48ltrs 666ml	222. 13km 140m
155. 50tonnes 692kg	189. 9ltrs 193ml	223. 18km 505m
156. 21 tonnes 350kg	190. 5ltrs 942ml	224. 14km 215m
157. 20kg 120g	191. 8ltrs 604ml	225. 12m 46cm
158. 45tonnes 109kg	192. 5ltrs 294ml	226. 23m 98cm
159. 32kg 145g	193. 21ltrs 462ml	227. 83m 62cm
160. 16tonnes 440kg	194. 22ltrs 389ml	228. 7m 34cm
161. 5ltrs 430ml	195. 6ltrs 195ml	229. 7km 805m
162. 1ltr 0ml	196. 40ltrs 977ml	230. 17km 105m
163. 8ltrs 900ml	197. 21ltrs 298ml	231. 53km 620m
164. 16ltrs 400ml	198. 26ltrs 888ml	232. 60km 775m
165. 12ltrs 475ml	199. 28ltrs 340ml	233. 8m 11cm
166. 10ltrs 960ml	200. 28ltrs 286ml	234. 12m 63cm
167. 1ltr 765ml	201. 1km 500m	235. 17m 17cm
168. 3ltrs 782ml	202. 3km 200m	236. 18m 63cm
169. 5ltrs 500ml	203. 3km 550m	237. 91m 90cm
170. 5ltrs 10ml	204. 6km 110m	238. 36km 212m
171. 9ltrs 736ml	205. 2km 30m	239. 32km 920m
172. 18ltrs 610ml	206. 2m 57cm	240. 34m 61cm
173. 5ltrs 285ml	207. 1m 25cm	241. $\frac{2}{4}$ $\left(\frac{1}{2}\right)$
174. 3ltrs 515ml	208. 2m 33cm	242. $\frac{2}{8}$ $\left(\frac{1}{4}\right)$
		243. $\frac{4}{6}$ $\left(\frac{2}{3}\right)$

Answers (continued)

244. $\frac{2}{9}$

245. $\frac{3}{8}$

246. $\frac{3}{8}$

247. $\frac{1}{6}$

248. $\frac{3}{7}$

249. $\frac{2}{6}$ $\left(\frac{1}{3}\right)$

250. $\frac{3}{12}$ $\left(\frac{1}{4}\right)$

251. $\frac{2}{9}$

252. $\frac{2}{12}$ $\left(\frac{1}{6}\right)$

253. $\frac{7}{10}$

254. $\frac{3}{10}$

255. $\frac{1}{12}$

256. $\frac{4}{9}$

257. $\frac{7}{16}$

258. $\frac{1}{16}$

259. $\frac{5}{14}$

260. $\frac{7}{16}$

261. $\frac{1}{2}$

262. $2\frac{1}{4}$

263. $1\frac{3}{4}$

264. $3\frac{2}{3}$

265. $1\frac{1}{6}$

266. $2\frac{1}{3}$

267. $4\frac{8}{9}$

268. $1\frac{5}{8}$

269. $1\frac{1}{4}$

270. $2\frac{1}{4}$

271. $3\frac{1}{3}$

272. $2\frac{4}{8}$ $\left(2\frac{1}{2}\right)$

273. $2\frac{7}{8}$

274. $4\frac{3}{12}$ $\left(4\frac{1}{4}\right)$

275. $6\frac{1}{12}$

276. $2\frac{1}{10}$

277. $7\frac{1}{6}$

278. $3\frac{1}{16}$

279. $2\frac{2}{9}$

280. $7\frac{9}{12}$ $\left(7\frac{3}{4}\right)$

281. $\frac{1}{4}$

282. $\frac{5}{12}$

283. $\frac{1}{10}$

284. $\frac{1}{12}$

285. $\frac{1}{12}$

286. $\frac{1}{6}$

287. $\frac{1}{12}$

288. $\frac{7}{12}$

289. $\frac{1}{24}$

290. $\frac{1}{14}$

291. $\frac{1}{12}$

292. $\frac{5}{18}$

293. $\frac{9}{20}$

294. $\frac{13}{24}$

295. $\frac{5}{24}$

296. $\frac{3}{10}$

297. $\frac{1}{18}$

298. $\frac{9}{16}$

299. $\frac{5}{18}$

300. $\frac{2}{15}$

301-340

–	10	12	14	16	18	20	22	24
2	8	10	12	14	16	18	20	22
4	6	8	10	12	14	16	18	20
6	4	6	8	10	12	14	16	18
8	2	4	6	8	10	12	14	16
10	0	2	4	6	8	10	12	14

341-370

–	129	256	384	472	532
19	110	237	365	453	513
21	108	235	363	451	511
23	106	233	361	449	509
25	104	231	359	447	507
27	102	229	357	445	505
29	100	227	355	443	503

371. 12

372. 5

373. 15

374. 20

375. 2

376. 2

377. 2

378. 10

379. 3

380. 10

381. 10

382. 1

383. 4

384. 10

385. 67

386. 12

387. 8

388. 1

389. 25

390. 7

391. 27

392. 55km

393. 527

394. 26

395. 9

396. 8

397. £128.41

398. 2hrs 10mins

399. £526.05

400. 24cm

161	ltrs	ml
	7	480
−	2	50

162	ltrs	ml
	6	500
−	5	500

163	ltrs	ml
	10	600
−	1	700

164	ltrs	ml
	20	300
−	3	900

165	ltrs	ml
	19	295
−	6	820

166	ltrs	ml
	13	460
−	2	500

167	ltrs	ml
	14	368
−	12	603

168	ltrs	ml
	11	891
−	8	109

169	ltrs	ml
	16	
−	10	500

170	ltrs	ml
	12	350
−	7	340

171	ltrs	ml
	24	137
−	14	401

172	ltrs	ml
	34	584
−	15	974

178	ltrs	ml
	42	573
−	37	288

174	ltrs	ml
	26	800
−	23	285

175	ltrs	ml
	8	490
−	6	300

176	ltrs	ml
	9	580
−	2	750

177	ltrs	ml
	15	150
−	3	120

178	ltrs	ml
	19	600
−	11	700

179	ltrs	ml
	12	200
−	7	56

180	ltrs	ml
	16	800
−	5	240

181	ltrs	ml	182	ltrs	ml	183	ltrs	ml	184	ltrs	ml
	17	285		12	600		36	430		43	39
	− 16	501		− 4	200		− 28	911		− 31	654

185	ltrs	ml	186	ltrs	ml	187	ltrs	ml	188	ltrs	ml
	54	859		67	507		89	245		102	613
	− 41	317		− 25	296		− 65	820		− 53	947

189	ltrs	ml	190	ltrs	ml	191	ltrs	ml	192	ltrs	ml
	17	245		35	242		30	752		62	827
	− 8	52		− 29	300		− 22	148		− 57	533

193	ltrs	ml	194	ltrs	ml	195	ltrs	ml	196	ltrs	ml
	74	406		48	210		100	812		82	691
	− 52	944		− 25	821		− 94	617		− 41	714

197	ltrs	ml	198	ltrs	ml	199	ltrs	ml	200	ltrs	ml
	38	421		50	634		96	849		118	713
	− 17	123		− 23	746		− 68	509		− 90	427

	km	m		km	m		km	m		km	m
201	3	200	202	5	600	203	7	300	204	9	990
	− 1	700		− 2	400		− 3	750		− 3	880

	km	m		m	cm		m	cm		m	cm
205	4	225	206	11	50	207	10	63	208	12	41
	− 2	195		− 8	93		− 9	38		−10	8

	km	m		km	m		km	m		km	m
209	4	220	210	6	960	211	7	970	212	5	60
	− 3	0		− 1	720		− 2	350		− 4	990

	m	cm		m	cm		m	cm		m	cm
213	10	52	214	8	60	215	9	77	216	12	38
	− 6	34		− 4	10		− 5	98		− 2	97

	km	m		km	m		m	cm		m	cm
217	5	490	218	9	500	219	7	60	220	11	45
	− 2	200		− 8	350		− 3	28		−10	82

221	km	m	222	km	m	223	km	m	224	km	m
	15	310		26	620		39	845		64	955
	− 2	160		−13	480		−21	340		−50	740

225	m	cm	226	m	cm	227	m	cm	228	m	cm
	42	16		62	49		97	83		84	32
	−29	70		−38	51		−14	21		−76	98

229	km	m	230	km	m	231	km	m	232	km	m
	44	920		32	65		78	250		110	285
	−37	115		−14	960		−24	630		− 49	510

233	m	cm	234	m	cm	235	m	cm	236	m	cm
	28	67		67	34		69	69		108	57
	−20	56		−54	71		−52	52		− 89	94

237	m	cm	238	km	m	239	km	m	240	m	cm
	131	14		53	510		98	680		84	90
	− 39	24		−17	298		−65	760		−50	29

241   $\dfrac{3}{4} - \dfrac{1}{4} =$ [ ]

242   $\dfrac{5}{8} - \dfrac{3}{8} =$ [ ]

243   $\dfrac{5}{6} - \dfrac{1}{6} =$ [ ]

244   $\dfrac{7}{9} - \dfrac{5}{9} =$ [ ]

245   $\dfrac{7}{8} - \dfrac{4}{8} =$ [ ]

246   $\dfrac{5}{8} - \dfrac{2}{8} =$ [ ]

247   $\dfrac{5}{6} - \dfrac{4}{6} =$ [ ]

248   $\dfrac{6}{7} - \dfrac{3}{7} =$ [ ]

249   $\dfrac{3}{6} - \dfrac{1}{6} =$ [ ]

250   $\dfrac{7}{12} - \dfrac{4}{12} =$ [ ]

251   $\dfrac{8}{9} - \dfrac{6}{9} =$ [ ]

252   $\dfrac{5}{12} - \dfrac{3}{12} =$ [ ]

253   $\dfrac{9}{10} - \dfrac{2}{10} =$ [ ]

254   $\dfrac{7}{10} - \dfrac{4}{10} =$ [ ]

255   $\dfrac{11}{12} - \dfrac{10}{12} =$ [ ]

256   $\dfrac{7}{9} - \dfrac{3}{9} =$ [ ]

257   $\dfrac{8}{16} - \dfrac{1}{16} =$ [ ]

258   $\dfrac{4}{16} - \dfrac{3}{16} =$ [ ]

259   $\dfrac{9}{14} - \dfrac{4}{14} =$ [ ]

260   $\dfrac{10}{16} - \dfrac{3}{16} =$ [ ]

261 $1 - \frac{1}{2} =$

262 $3 - \frac{3}{4} =$

263 $2 - \frac{1}{4} =$

264 $4 - \frac{1}{3} =$

265 $2 - \frac{5}{6} =$

266 $5 - 2\frac{2}{3} =$

267 $8 - 3\frac{1}{9} =$

268 $6 - 4\frac{3}{8} =$

269 $2\frac{1}{2} - 1\frac{1}{4} =$

270 $3\frac{3}{4} - 1\frac{2}{4} =$

271 $4\frac{2}{3} - 1\frac{1}{3} =$

272 $6\frac{7}{8} - 4\frac{3}{8} =$

273 $5\frac{3}{8} - 2\frac{4}{8} =$

274 $8\frac{7}{12} - 4\frac{4}{12} =$

275 $7\frac{6}{12} - 1\frac{5}{12} =$

276 $4\frac{9}{10} - 2\frac{8}{10} =$

277 $9\frac{2}{6} - 2\frac{1}{6} =$

278 $6\frac{11}{16} - 3\frac{10}{16} =$

279 $5\frac{5}{9} - 3\frac{3}{9} =$

280 $8\frac{10}{12} - 1\frac{1}{12} =$

281 $\dfrac{3}{4} - \dfrac{1}{2} =$

282 $\dfrac{2}{3} - \dfrac{1}{4} =$

283 $\dfrac{1}{2} - \dfrac{2}{5} =$

284 $\dfrac{5}{6} - \dfrac{3}{4} =$

285 $\dfrac{3}{4} - \dfrac{2}{3} =$ 291 $\dfrac{1}{3} - \dfrac{1}{4} =$

286 $\dfrac{2}{3} - \dfrac{1}{2} =$ 292 $\dfrac{7}{9} - \dfrac{1}{2} =$

287 $\dfrac{1}{4} - \dfrac{1}{6} =$ 293 $\dfrac{7}{10} - \dfrac{1}{4} =$

288 $\dfrac{3}{4} - \dfrac{1}{6} =$ 294 $\dfrac{2}{3} - \dfrac{1}{8} =$

289 $\dfrac{1}{6} - \dfrac{1}{8} =$ 295 $\dfrac{5}{8} - \dfrac{5}{12} =$

290 $\dfrac{1}{2} - \dfrac{3}{7} =$ 296 $\dfrac{4}{5} - \dfrac{1}{2} =$

297 $\dfrac{8}{9} - \dfrac{5}{6} =$

298 $\dfrac{15}{16} - \dfrac{3}{8} =$

299 $\dfrac{4}{9} - \dfrac{1}{6} =$

300 $\dfrac{4}{5} - \dfrac{2}{3} =$

21

301-340

−	10	12	14	16	18	20	22	24
2								
4								
6								
8								
10								

341-370

−	129	256	384	472	532
19					
21					
23					
25					
27					
29					

Find n.

n =

371   n   =   15 − 3

372   2n   =   20 − 10

373   n   =   20 − 5

374   4n   =   100 − 20

375   7n   =   34 − 20

376   5n   =   15 − 5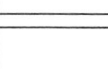

377   6n   =   24 − 12

378   2n   =   32 − 12

379   10n   =   40 − 10

380   3n   =   100 − 70

381   2n   =   30 − 10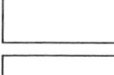

382   5n   =   10 − 5

383   4n   =   36 − 20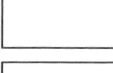

384   10n   =   120 − 20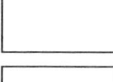

385   n   =   76 − 9

386   12n   =   244 − 100

387   5n   =   60 − 20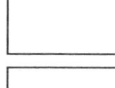

388   2n   =   20 − 18

389   4n   =   212 − 112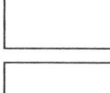

390   3n   =   77 − 56

391 Alan is 7, his dad is 34. What is the difference in their ages? _____

392 Dad's car journey from home to Newark is 73 km.
He stops at Lincoln for petrol. The distance between
Lincoln and Newark is 18 km. How far has he travelled? _____

393 Desmond had saved 973 computer tokens towards a computer
which cost 1500. How many more does he need to collect? _____

394 Julie and Kate planted 49 tulip bulbs and 97 daffodil bulbs.
120 flowers grew. How many bulbs did not grow? _____

A shopkeeper bought 2 dozen boxes of Cornflakes and 3
dozen boxes of Krispies. He sold 15 boxes of Cornflakes
and 28 boxes of Krispies.

395 How many boxes of Cornflakes does he have left? _____

396 How many boxes of Krispies does he have left? _____

397 William has three bank accounts. In the first he has £241.80,
in the second he has £127.75 and in the third £86.36.
He buys a bicycle for £327.50. How much money has he left? _____

398 The children have to have 5 hours 25mins of lessons a day.
Maths lasts 1 hour 30mins and Technology lasts 1 hour 45mins.
How long is left to share between English, French and PE? _____

399 Kathryn wins £1000 in a painting competition. She gives £350
to her brother and spends £123.95 on some new clothes.
How much has she left? _____

400 The Brown family need some new curtains. Their windows
measure 2 metres, 1 metre 24cm and 98cms. Mr Brown
buys 3 metres 98cm of curtain material.
How much more material should he have bought? _____